I'M SO FREAKING FREAKED OUT

KNOCK KNOCK®
VENICE, CALIFORNIA

Created, published, and distributed by Knock Knock
1635-B Electric Ave.
Venice, CA 90291
knockknockstuff.com
Knock Knock is a registered trademark of Knock Knock LLC

ISBN: 978-160106884-2
UPC: 825703-50098-1

10 9 8 7 6 5 4 3 2 1

DATE		

WHY I'M SO FREAKING FREAKED OUT TODAY:

_____

_____

_____

_____

_____

_____

_____

_____

_____

_____

_____

_____

_____

_____

_____

_____

_____

_____

TODAY'S STRESS LEVEL:

He was alone with his thoughts.
They were extremely unpleasant
thoughts and he would rather
have had a chaperon.

Douglas Adams

DATE		

WHY I'M SO FREAKING FREAKED OUT TODAY:

_____

_____

_____

_____

_____

_____

_____

_____

_____

_____

_____

_____

_____

_____

_____

_____

_____

_____

_____

_____

_____

TODAY'S STRESS LEVEL:

"Blorft" is an adjective I just made up that means "Completely overwhelmed but proceeding as if everything is fine and reacting to the stress with the torpor of a possum."

Tina Fey

DATE		

WHY I'M SO FREAKING FREAKED OUT TODAY:

_____

_____

_____

_____

_____

_____

_____

_____

_____

_____

_____

_____

_____

_____

_____

_____

_____

_____

TODAY'S STRESS LEVEL:

There's nothing wrong with fear; the only mistake is to let it stop you in your tracks.

Twyla Tharp

DATE

WHY I'M SO FREAKING FREAKED OUT TODAY:

_____

_____

_____

_____

_____

_____

_____

_____

_____

_____

_____

_____

_____

_____

_____

_____

_____

TODAY'S STRESS LEVEL:

In a dark time, the eye begins to see.

Theodore Roethke

WHY I'M SO FREAKING FREAKED OUT TODAY:

_____

_____

_____

_____

_____

_____

_____

_____

_____

_____

_____

_____

_____

_____

_____

_____

_____

TODAY'S STRESS LEVEL:

A jewel's just a rock put under enormous heat and pressure. Extraordinary things are always hiding in places people never think to look.

Jodi Picoult

	DATE	

WHY I'M SO FREAKING FREAKED OUT TODAY:

_____

_____

_____

_____

_____

_____

_____

_____

_____

_____

_____

_____

_____

_____

_____

_____

_____

_____

_____

TODAY'S STRESS LEVEL:

My ordinary state of mind
is very much like the
waiting room at the DMV.

Leonard Cohen

DATE		

WHY I'M SO FREAKING FREAKED OUT TODAY:

_____

_____

_____

_____

_____

_____

_____

_____

_____

_____

_____

_____

_____

_____

_____

_____

TODAY'S STRESS LEVEL:

I feel like I could
throw off sparks,
or break a window—
maybe rearrange
all the furniture.

Raymond Carver

DATE		

WHY I'M SO FREAKING FREAKED OUT TODAY:

_____

_____

_____

_____

_____

_____

_____

_____

_____

_____

_____

_____

_____

_____

_____

_____

_____

TODAY'S STRESS LEVEL:

We are in many many troubles
for the moment, so many that
grief loses its dignity and bursts
out laughing.

Robert Frost

DATE

WHY I'M SO FREAKING FREAKED OUT TODAY:

_____

_____

_____

_____

_____

_____

_____

_____

_____

_____

_____

_____

_____

_____

_____

_____

_____

_____

_____

TODAY'S STRESS LEVEL:

Life is difficult, and complicated and beyond anyone's total control, and the humility to know that will enable you to survive its vicissitudes.

J. K. Rowling

WHY I'M SO FREAKING FREAKED OUT TODAY:

_____

_____

_____

_____

_____

_____

_____

_____

_____

_____

_____

_____

_____

_____

_____

_____

_____

TODAY'S STRESS LEVEL:

And when things start to happen,
don't worry. Don't stew.
Just go right along.
You'll start happening too.

Dr. Seuss

DATE

WHY I'M SO FREAKING FREAKED OUT TODAY:

_____

_____

_____

_____

_____

_____

_____

_____

_____

_____

_____

_____

_____

_____

_____

_____

_____

_____

TODAY'S STRESS LEVEL:

Quite collected at cocktail parties,
meanwhile in my head
I'm undergoing open-heart surgery.

Anne Sexton

DATE		

WHY I'M SO FREAKING FREAKED OUT TODAY:

_____

_____

_____

_____

_____

_____

_____

_____

_____

_____

_____

_____

_____

_____

_____

_____

_____

_____

TODAY'S STRESS LEVEL:

In the dark times
Will there also be
   singing?
Yes, there will also be
   singing
About the dark times.

Bertolt Brecht

WHY I'M SO FREAKING FREAKED OUT TODAY:

_____

_____

_____

_____

_____

_____

_____

_____

_____

_____

_____

_____

_____

_____

_____

_____

_____

_____

_____

TODAY'S STRESS LEVEL:

I found the third grade to be very stressful academically.

Jonathan Ames

DATE		

WHY I'M SO FREAKING FREAKED OUT TODAY:

_____

_____

_____

_____

_____

_____

_____

_____

_____

_____

_____

_____

_____

_____

_____

_____

_____

_____

_____

_____

_____

TODAY'S STRESS LEVEL:

The ultimate measure of a man is not where he stands in moments of comfort and convenience, but where he stands at times of challenge and controversy.

Martin Luther King, Jr.

DATE		

WHY I'M SO FREAKING FREAKED OUT TODAY:

_____

_____

_____

_____

_____

_____

_____

_____

_____

_____

_____

_____

_____

_____

_____

_____

_____

_____

_____

TODAY'S STRESS LEVEL:

I have
woven a
parachute
out of
everything
broken.

William Stafford

DATE		

WHY I'M SO FREAKING FREAKED OUT TODAY:

_____

_____

_____

_____

_____

_____

_____

_____

_____

_____

_____

_____

_____

_____

_____

_____

TODAY'S STRESS LEVEL:

This sounds so bleak when I say it, but we need some delusions to keep us going. And the people who successfully delude themselves seem happier than the people who can't.

Woody Allen

	DATE	

WHY I'M SO FREAKING FREAKED OUT TODAY:

_____

_____

_____

_____

_____

_____

_____

_____

_____

_____

_____

_____

_____

_____

_____

_____

TODAY'S STRESS LEVEL:

Woe-is-me is not an attractive narrative.

Maureen Dowd

DATE		

WHY I'M SO FREAKING FREAKED OUT TODAY:

_____

_____

_____

_____

_____

_____

_____

_____

_____

_____

_____

_____

_____

_____

_____

_____

_____

_____

TODAY'S STRESS LEVEL:

In times of great stress and adversity, it's always best to keep busy, to plow your anger and your energy into something positive.

Lee Iacocca

DATE		

WHY I'M SO FREAKING FREAKED OUT TODAY:

_____

_____

_____

_____

_____

_____

_____

_____

_____

_____

_____

_____

_____

_____

_____

_____

_____

TODAY'S STRESS LEVEL:

What if you do fail, and get fairly rolled in the dirt once or twice? Up again, you shall never be so afraid of a tumble.

Ralph Waldo Emerson

WHY I'M SO FREAKING FREAKED OUT TODAY:

_____

_____

_____

_____

_____

_____

_____

_____

_____

_____

_____

_____

_____

_____

_____

_____

_____

TODAY'S STRESS LEVEL:

There must be quite a few things that a hot bath won't cure, but I don't know many of them.

Sylvia Plath

WHY I'M SO FREAKING FREAKED OUT TODAY:

_____

_____

_____

_____

_____

_____

_____

_____

_____

_____

_____

_____

_____

_____

_____

TODAY'S STRESS LEVEL:

Every time you are tempted to react in the same old way, ask if you want to be a prisoner of the past or a pioneer of the future.

Deepak Chopra

WHY I'M SO FREAKING FREAKED OUT TODAY:

_____

_____

_____

_____

_____

_____

_____

_____

_____

_____

_____

_____

_____

_____

_____

_____

TODAY'S STRESS LEVEL:

Panic—a deep abiding, free-floating anxiety, often without any reason or logical basis.

Nelson Demille

DATE

WHY I'M SO FREAKING FREAKED OUT TODAY:

_____

_____

_____

_____

_____

_____

_____

_____

_____

_____

_____

_____

_____

_____

_____

_____

_____

TODAY'S STRESS LEVEL:

I fail and I go on. Failure is a beginning, failure is the springboard of hope.

Carla Needleman

WHY I'M SO FREAKING FREAKED OUT TODAY:

_____

_____

_____

_____

_____

_____

_____

_____

_____

_____

_____

_____

_____

_____

_____

_____

_____

_____

TODAY'S STRESS LEVEL:

To allow oneself to be carried away by a multitude of conflicting concerns, to surrender to too many demands, to commit oneself to too many projects, to want to help everyone in everything is to succumb to violence.

Thomas Merton

DATE

WHY I'M SO FREAKING FREAKED OUT TODAY:

_____

_____

_____

_____

_____

_____

_____

_____

_____

_____

_____

_____

_____

_____

_____

_____

_____

TODAY'S STRESS LEVEL:

I've got to start listening to those quiet, nagging doubts.

Bill Watterson

	DATE	

WHY I'M SO FREAKING FREAKED OUT TODAY:

_____

_____

_____

_____

_____

_____

_____

_____

_____

_____

_____

_____

_____

_____

_____

_____

TODAY'S STRESS LEVEL:

Our doubt is our passion and our passion is our task. The rest is the madness of art.

Henry James

WHY I'M SO FREAKING FREAKED OUT TODAY:

_____

_____

_____

_____

_____

_____

_____

_____

_____

_____

_____

_____

_____

_____

_____

_____

_____

TODAY'S STRESS LEVEL:

To think you can change your life by changing its outward conditions is just like thinking, as I did as a boy, that by sitting on a stick and taking hold of it at both ends I could lift myself up.

Leo Tolstoy

DATE		

WHY I'M SO FREAKING FREAKED OUT TODAY:

_____

_____

_____

_____

_____

_____

_____

_____

_____

_____

_____

_____

_____

_____

_____

_____

_____

_____

_____

TODAY'S STRESS LEVEL:

You may not control all the events that happen to you, but you can decide not to be reduced by them.

Maya Angelou

DATE

WHY I'M SO FREAKING FREAKED OUT TODAY:

_____

_____

_____

_____

_____

_____

_____

_____

_____

_____

_____

_____

_____

_____

_____

_____

_____

TODAY'S STRESS LEVEL:

I'd love to tell you I had some deep revelation on my way down, that I came to terms with my own mortality, laughed in the face of death, et cetera.

The truth? My only thought was: Aaaaggghhhhh!

Rick Riordan

DATE		

WHY I'M SO FREAKING FREAKED OUT TODAY:

_____

_____

_____

_____

_____

_____

_____

_____

_____

_____

_____

_____

_____

_____

_____

_____

_____

_____

TODAY'S STRESS LEVEL:

It is a common experience that a problem difficult at night is resolved in the morning after the committee of sleep has worked on it.

John Steinback

WHY I'M SO FREAKING FREAKED OUT TODAY:

_____

_____

_____

_____

_____

_____

_____

_____

_____

_____

_____

_____

_____

_____

_____

_____

TODAY'S STRESS LEVEL:

Sometimes the most intelligent thing
is not to do anything, certainly
nothing loaded with the imbecility
of emotionality.

William Saroyan

DATE		

WHY I'M SO FREAKING FREAKED OUT TODAY:

_____

_____

_____

_____

_____

_____

_____

_____

_____

_____

_____

_____

_____

_____

_____

_____

_____

_____

_____

TODAY'S STRESS LEVEL:

My mind turned by anxiety, or other cause, from its scrutiny of blank paper, is like a lost child—wandering the house, sitting on the bottom step to cry.

Virginia Woolf

WHY I'M SO FREAKING FREAKED OUT TODAY:

_____

_____

_____

_____

_____

_____

_____

_____

_____

_____

_____

_____

_____

_____

_____

_____

_____

TODAY'S STRESS LEVEL:

I write to
explore
all the
things I'm
afraid of.

Joss Whedon

WHY I'M SO FREAKING FREAKED OUT TODAY:

_____

_____

_____

_____

_____

_____

_____

_____

_____

_____

_____

_____

_____

_____

_____

_____

_____

_____

_____

TODAY'S STRESS LEVEL:

Outer order contributes to inner calm.

Gretchen Rubin

DATE		

WHY I'M SO FREAKING FREAKED OUT TODAY:

_____

_____

_____

_____

_____

_____

_____

_____

_____

_____

_____

_____

_____

_____

_____

_____

_____

_____

TODAY'S STRESS LEVEL:

You can tell a lot from a person's nails. When a life starts to unravel, they're among the first to go.

Ian McEwan

DATE

WHY I'M SO FREAKING FREAKED OUT TODAY:

_____

_____

_____

_____

_____

_____

_____

_____

_____

_____

_____

_____

_____

_____

_____

_____

_____

TODAY'S STRESS LEVEL:

Fear is the mind-killer.

Frank Herbert

WHY I'M SO FREAKING FREAKED OUT TODAY:

_____

_____

_____

_____

_____

_____

_____

_____

_____

_____

_____

_____

_____

_____

_____

_____

_____

_____

TODAY'S STRESS LEVEL:

But we also know that only those who dare to fail greatly, can ever achieve greatly.

Robert F. Kennedy

	DATE		

WHY I'M SO FREAKING FREAKED OUT TODAY:

_____

_____

_____

_____

_____

_____

_____

_____

_____

_____

_____

_____

_____

_____

_____

_____

_____

_____

TODAY'S STRESS LEVEL:

Unease, anxiety, tension, stress, worry—all forms of fear—are caused by too much future, and not enough presence.

Eckhart Tolle

DATE		

WHY I'M SO FREAKING FREAKED OUT TODAY:

_____

_____

_____

_____

_____

_____

_____

_____

_____

_____

_____

_____

_____

_____

_____

_____

_____

_____

TODAY'S STRESS LEVEL:

Anxiety and Ennui are the Scylla and Charybdis on which the bark of human happiness is most commonly wrecked.

William Edward Hartpole Lecky

DATE

WHY I'M SO FREAKING FREAKED OUT TODAY:

_____

_____

_____

_____

_____

_____

_____

_____

_____

_____

_____

_____

_____

_____

_____

_____

_____

_____

TODAY'S STRESS LEVEL:

Now
That
All your worry
Has proved such an
Unlucrative
Business,
Why
Not
Find a better
Job.

Hafiz

	DATE	

WHY I'M SO FREAKING FREAKED OUT TODAY:

_____

_____

_____

_____

_____

_____

_____

_____

_____

_____

_____

_____

_____

_____

_____

_____

_____

TODAY'S STRESS LEVEL:

Let everything happen to you:
beauty and terror.
Only press on: no feeling is final.

Rainer Maria Rilke

WHY I'M SO FREAKING FREAKED OUT TODAY:

_____

_____

_____

_____

_____

_____

_____

_____

_____

_____

_____

_____

_____

_____

_____

_____

TODAY'S STRESS LEVEL:

You know what a thorough sufferer
I can be. I not only hit bottom, I walk
for miles and miles on it.

Saul Bellow

DATE

WHY I'M SO FREAKING FREAKED OUT TODAY:

_____

_____

_____

_____

_____

_____

_____

_____

_____

_____

_____

_____

_____

_____

_____

_____

_____

_____

TODAY'S STRESS LEVEL:

I really don't know what to do when my life is not chaotic.

Carrie Brownstein

WHY I'M SO FREAKING FREAKED OUT TODAY:

_____

_____

_____

_____

_____

_____

_____

_____

_____

_____

_____

_____

_____

_____

_____

_____

_____

_____

TODAY'S STRESS LEVEL:

We are frazzled and unruly, you and me. We are desperate and wistful and restless and funny and frayed at the edges.

Heather Havrilesky

WHY I'M SO FREAKING FREAKED OUT TODAY:

_____

_____

_____

_____

_____

_____

_____

_____

_____

_____

_____

_____

_____

_____

_____

_____

_____

_____

_____

TODAY'S STRESS LEVEL:

Let the peace of this day be here tomorrow when I wake up.

Thomas Pynchon

DATE		

WHY I'M SO FREAKING FREAKED OUT TODAY:

_____

_____

_____

_____

_____

_____

_____

_____

_____

_____

_____

_____

_____

_____

_____

_____

_____

_____

TODAY'S STRESS LEVEL:

We live only a few conscious decades, and we fret ourselves enough for several lifetimes.

Chrisopher Hitchens

DATE

WHY I'M SO FREAKING FREAKED OUT TODAY:

_____

_____

_____

_____

_____

_____

_____

_____

_____

_____

_____

_____

_____

_____

_____

_____

_____

_____

_____

_____

TODAY'S STRESS LEVEL:

Fear is contagious.
You can catch it.
Sometimes all it
takes is for someone
to say that they're
scared for the fear to
become real.

Neil Gaiman

WHY I'M SO FREAKING FREAKED OUT TODAY:

_____

_____

_____

_____

_____

_____

_____

_____

_____

_____

_____

_____

_____

_____

_____

_____

_____

TODAY'S STRESS LEVEL:

It's not time to worry yet.

Harper Lee

WHY I'M SO FREAKING FREAKED OUT TODAY:

_____

_____

_____

_____

_____

_____

_____

_____

_____

_____

_____

_____

_____

_____

_____

_____

_____

_____

TODAY'S STRESS LEVEL:

I am often 15 minutes late because of my inexplicable anxiety about being 2 minutes early.

B. J. Novak

DATE

WHY I'M SO FREAKING FREAKED OUT TODAY:

_____

_____

_____

_____

_____

_____

_____

_____

_____

_____

_____

_____

_____

_____

_____

_____

_____

_____

TODAY'S STRESS LEVEL:

But we wouldn't
do much if we didn't
do things that nobody
ever heard of before.

Laura Ingalls Wilder

WHY I'M SO FREAKING FREAKED OUT TODAY:

_____

_____

_____

_____

_____

_____

_____

_____

_____

_____

_____

_____

_____

_____

_____

_____

_____

_____

_____

TODAY'S STRESS LEVEL:

There's a plague inside of me /
Eating at my disposition /
Nothing's left

Green Day

WHY I'M SO FREAKING FREAKED OUT TODAY:

_____

_____

_____

_____

_____

_____

_____

_____

_____

_____

_____

_____

_____

_____

_____

_____

TODAY'S STRESS LEVEL:

The social barriers in life are so intense and horrific that every encounter is just fraught with so many problems and dread. Every situation is a potential nightmare.

Larry David

DATE		

WHY I'M SO FREAKING FREAKED OUT TODAY:

_____

_____

_____

_____

_____

_____

_____

_____

_____

_____

_____

_____

_____

_____

_____

_____

_____

_____

TODAY'S STRESS LEVEL:

Disaster is virtue's opportunity.

Seneca

DATE		

WHY I'M SO FREAKING FREAKED OUT TODAY:

_____

_____

_____

_____

_____

_____

_____

_____

_____

_____

_____

_____

_____

_____

_____

_____

_____

_____

TODAY'S STRESS LEVEL:

The disturbers of happiness, in this world, are our desires, our griefs, and our fears.

Samuel Johnson

WHY I'M SO FREAKING FREAKED OUT TODAY:

_____

_____

_____

_____

_____

_____

_____

_____

_____

_____

_____

_____

_____

_____

_____

_____

_____

_____

_____

TODAY'S STRESS LEVEL:

Drag your thoughts away from your troubles—by the ears, by the heels, or any other way, so you manage it.

Mark Twain

DATE		

WHY I'M SO FREAKING FREAKED OUT TODAY:

_____

_____

_____

_____

_____

_____

_____

_____

_____

_____

_____

_____

_____

_____

_____

_____

_____

TODAY'S STRESS LEVEL:

Failure after long perseverance is much grander than never to have a striving good enough to be called a failure.

George Eliot

WHY I'M SO FREAKING FREAKED OUT TODAY:

_____

_____

_____

_____

_____

_____

_____

_____

_____

_____

_____

_____

_____

_____

_____

_____

_____

_____

TODAY'S STRESS LEVEL:

When we are angry or frightened it is not by our choice; but our virtues are expressions of our choice, or at any rate imply choice.

Aristotle

DATE		

WHY I'M SO FREAKING FREAKED OUT TODAY:

_____

_____

_____

_____

_____

_____

_____

_____

_____

_____

_____

_____

_____

_____

_____

_____

_____

TODAY'S STRESS LEVEL:

Ever been in a spelling bee as a kid? That snowy second after the announcement of the word as you sift your brain to see if you can spell it? It was like that, the blank panic.

Gillian Flynn

WHY I'M SO FREAKING FREAKED OUT TODAY:

_____

_____

_____

_____

_____

_____

_____

_____

_____

_____

_____

_____

_____

_____

_____

_____

_____

_____

TODAY'S STRESS LEVEL:

Anxiety is love's greatest killer, because it is like the stranglehold of the drowning.

Anaïs Nin

WHY I'M SO FREAKING FREAKED OUT TODAY:

_____

_____

_____

_____

_____

_____

_____

_____

_____

_____

_____

_____

_____

_____

_____

_____

TODAY'S STRESS LEVEL:

Scary, isn't it? But what wonderful thing didn't start out scary?

Isaac Marion

DATE		

WHY I'M SO FREAKING FREAKED OUT TODAY:

_____

_____

_____

_____

_____

_____

_____

_____

_____

_____

_____

_____

_____

_____

_____

_____

_____

_____

TODAY'S STRESS LEVEL:

The world breaks
everyone and afterward
many are strong at the
broken places.

Ernest Hemingway

DATE		

WHY I'M SO FREAKING FREAKED OUT TODAY:

_____

_____

_____

_____

_____

_____

_____

_____

_____

_____

_____

_____

_____

_____

_____

_____

_____

_____

_____

TODAY'S STRESS LEVEL:

Each of us has his own rhythm of suffering.

Roland Barthes

DATE		

WHY I'M SO FREAKING FREAKED OUT TODAY:

_____

_____

_____

_____

_____

_____

_____

_____

_____

_____

_____

_____

_____

_____

_____

_____

_____

_____

_____

TODAY'S STRESS LEVEL:

When it finally briefly happens, happiness can feel very worrying.

Alain de Botton

DATE

WHY I'M SO FREAKING FREAKED OUT TODAY:

_____

_____

_____

_____

_____

_____

_____

_____

_____

_____

_____

_____

_____

_____

_____

_____

TODAY'S STRESS LEVEL:

Just breathing can
be such a luxury
sometimes.

Walter Kirn

WHY I'M SO FREAKING FREAKED OUT TODAY:

_____

_____

_____

_____

_____

_____

_____

_____

_____

_____

_____

_____

_____

_____

_____

_____

_____

TODAY'S STRESS LEVEL:

There is no such thing as inner peace.
There is only nervousness or death.

Fran Lebowitz

DATE

WHY I'M SO FREAKING FREAKED OUT TODAY:

_____

_____

_____

_____

_____

_____

_____

_____

_____

_____

_____

_____

_____

_____

_____

_____

_____

TODAY'S STRESS LEVEL:

Think of your
head as an unsafe
neighborhood;
don't go there alone.

Augusten Burroughs

WHY I'M SO FREAKING FREAKED OUT TODAY:

_____

_____

_____

_____

_____

_____

_____

_____

_____

_____

_____

_____

_____

_____

_____

_____

_____

TODAY'S STRESS LEVEL:

I will show you fear in a handful of dust.

T. S. Eliot

WHY I'M SO FREAKING FREAKED OUT TODAY:

_____

_____

_____

_____

_____

_____

_____

_____

_____

_____

_____

_____

_____

_____

_____

_____

_____

TODAY'S STRESS LEVEL:

Our real fears are the sounds of footsteps walking in the corridors of our minds, and the anxieties, the phantom floatings, they create.

Truman Capote

WHY I'M SO FREAKING FREAKED OUT TODAY:

_____

_____

_____

_____

_____

_____

_____

_____

_____

_____

_____

_____

_____

_____

_____

_____

_____

TODAY'S STRESS LEVEL:

I have a new philosophy. I'm only going to dread one day at a time.

Charles M. Schulz

WHY I'M SO FREAKING FREAKED OUT TODAY:

TODAY'S STRESS LEVEL:

If you have good thoughts they will shine out of your face like sunbeams and you will always look lovely.

Roald Dahl

DATE

WHY I'M SO FREAKING FREAKED OUT TODAY:

_____

_____

_____

_____

_____

_____

_____

_____

_____

_____

_____

_____

_____

_____

_____

_____

_____

_____

_____

TODAY'S STRESS LEVEL:

To be fully alive, fully human, and completely awake is to be continually thrown out of the nest.

Pema Chödrön

DATE

WHY I'M SO FREAKING FREAKED OUT TODAY:

_____

_____

_____

_____

_____

_____

_____

_____

_____

_____

_____

_____

_____

_____

_____

_____

_____

TODAY'S STRESS LEVEL:

I'm not afraid of storms, for I'm learning how to sail my ship.

Louisa May Alcott

	DATE	

WHY I'M SO FREAKING FREAKED OUT TODAY:

.

There's no place like om.

Knock Knock